Getting to the Green

GETTING TO THE GREEN

Golf, Financial Planning, and Life,
Not Necessarily in That Order

Altair M. Gobo, CFP®

U.S. Financial Services, L.L.C.

HIGHPOINT
EXECUTIVE
PUBLISHING

This edition published by Highpoint Executive Publishing.
For information, write to info@highpointpubs.com.

First Edition

ISBN: 978-0-9974157-3-5

Library of Congress Cataloging-in-Publication Data

Gobo, Altair M.
Getting to the Green: Golf, Financial Planning and Life, Not Necessarily in That Order
Includes index.

Summary: "Golf can be serious, and so are your finances. Getting to the Green takes a look at the many things that golf, financial planning, and (by extension) modern day life have in common. If you're a golfer, the comparisons may very well help to make the game become a little more significant to you. Even if you're not a golfer, this book will still help you to achieve financial success in life."– Provided by publisher.

ISBN: 978-0-9974157-3-5 (hardbound)
1.Business 2. Financial Planning

Library of Congress Control Number: 2016951771

Design by Sarah M. Clarehart

Manufactured in the United States of America
10 9 8 7 6 5 4 3 2 1

"Goodness is the only investment that never fails."
—HENRY DAVID THOREAU

"The tax on capital gains directly affects investment decisions, the mobility and flow of risk capital...the ease or difficulty experienced by new ventures in obtaining capital, and thereby the strength and potential for growth in the economy."
—JOHN F. KENNEDY

"No man needs sympathy because he has to work, because he has a burden to carry. Far and away the best prize that life offers is the chance to work hard at work worth doing."
—THEODORE ROOSEVELT

"A budget tells us what we can't afford, but it doesn't keep us from buying it."
—WILLIAM FEATHER

"At about the time we can make the ends meet, somebody moves the ends."
—HERBERT HOOVER

"An economist is an expert who will know tomorrow why the things he predicted yesterday didn't happen."
—LAURENCE J. PETER

"As a small businessman, you have no greater leverage than the truth."
—JOHN GREENLEAF WHITTIER

"In the business world, everyone is paid in two coins: cash and experience. Take the experience first; the cash will come later."
—HAROLD S. GENEEN

"Informed decision-making comes from a long tradition of guessing and then blaming others for inadequate results."
—SCOTT ADAMS

"It usually takes me more than three weeks to prepare a good impromptu speech."
—MARK TWAIN

"It's easy to make a buck. It's a lot tougher to make a difference."
—TOM BROKAW

"Our favorite holding period is forever."
—WARREN BUFFETT

"The hardest thing to understand in the world is the income tax."
—ALBERT EINSTEIN

"The invisible hand of the market always moves faster and better than the heavy hand of the government."
—MITT ROMNEY

"The meek shall inherit the Earth, but not its mineral rights."
—J. PAUL GETTY

"Whales only get harpooned when they come to the surface, and turtles can only move forward when they stick their neck out, but investors face risk no matter what they do."
—CHARLES A. JAFFE

Contents

Dedication

In my attempt to demystify the challenges of golf, wealth management, and life in general, I dedicate this book to all the weekend warriors who come out for a day of fun with their buddies to enjoy this wonderful game.

Hopefully, the demystification of wealth management will provide them, and you, with more time to play and live life today, while being confident about tomorrow!

Acknowledgments

To all the people in my life who have helped define me as the person I am today:

My wife, the eternal optimist, continues to make sure the glass is always more than half full; my sons who have taught me the true meaning of unconditional love; my brother, whom I miss dearly, who defined wealth by one's character rather than his bank account; my three sisters who reaffirm every day the importance of family; to the rest of my extended family who remain closer to me than ever.

I would also like to thank my partners and everyone at U.S. Financial Services, LLC for creating a work environment that is our "second home," committed to ensuring our clients are always treated with honesty, integrity and respect. By the way, we have the best clients in the world!

To my publisher who helped to keep me on track.

I would like to thank all the friends I have from childhood until now who have each, in their own way, taught me a life lesson.

I would also like to acknowledge those who are not my friends (some by choice) because they, too, have taught me that life is too short to focus on the negative.

To every golf pro who's had the patience to give me a lesson and help me gain a better appreciation for the game.

And finally, my golf buddies, old and new, who remind me every round that golf is a microcosm of life—that we are not alone in our trials and tribulations, and how, at the end of the day, it is important to put a smile on someone's face.

Prepare to Play

"The income tax has made more liars out of the American people than golf has."
— WILL ROGERS

I 'm a weekend golfer, and I love everything about the game: the beautiful scenery of the course, the camaraderie I forge with the people, the occasional "great shot." The more I play, take lessons, and speak with other golfers, the more I realize that what I have learned on the golf course also applies to my life—and to my career as a financial advisor.

Golf should, and can, be fun. It can also teach you a lot about financial planning and life itself. And, like life and wealth management, golf certainly has its frustrations and hard-won lessons.

No wonder that for decades, golf has been taking heat from others. Mark Twain called it "a wonderful way to ruin a pleasant walk." Some vaudevillian once said of golf: "That's where you put a little white ball on a tiny, colored piece of wood, hit it...and then the first one who finds the ball wins."

There certainly is no shortage of golf jokes. To say that there are thousands of them is a massive understatement. Some are irreverent, some are downright foul—but most of them are good-natured reflections of what, for most weekend golfers, is a party atmosphere.

Golf is a healthy exercise, a diversion, a distraction, a way to get away from life's pressures (by creating substitute pressures, some say). It can be a challenge that helps you keep sharp, a time killer, a time consumer, and more. Golf is for people of all ages: I've met kids and folks well into their 80s on the golf course. But whatever else it is, it is instructive and fun.

"Play a Round" or "Play Around"?

There are some major differences between golfers. Some simply regard golf as a "pleasant walk in the country with friends." For others, it's a sport that is taken very seriously—one that includes not only those inexplicably vested with natural talent and well-honed skills—but also people who have PGA handicaps, and who, with varying degrees of success, are trying to get those handicaps down to respectable levels.

So, in both golf and finances, you have to decide whether you want to "play a round" or simply "play around." If all you want is the latter, there certainly is nothing wrong with that. However, if that's the case, golf will have about as much meaning to you as would the experience of occasionally dropping a coin into a pinball machine. It won't offer much in the way of excitement or drama. Of course, you also won't be subjected to the frustration that bites at the middle-aged handicapper who can't stop slicing the ball, or who can't get out of a sand trap.

Golf and Financial Planning

It shouldn't come as a surprise that a large part of golf dynamics applies to financial life. For some people, "financial life" means counting the money in their wallets to see how they are doing. If they got the bills paid last month, they regard that as "doing pretty well." If they spent more than what was available, or more than they make, they're not doing so well, and they reach for their credit cards.

Those credit cards are too often used by those who think they are some kind of liquid asset. These people (and I'm sure you're not one of them) would rather "play around" than "play a round."

"A round" in the world of golf is usually 18 holes. "A round" in the world of personal finances is a lifetime, so it is a good idea to plan accordingly, and don't play around. Hey, golf can be serious, and so are your finances.

What Is Your Handicap?

When Sammy Davis Jr. was asked this question by his golf companions, his response was: "Well, I'm black, Jewish, and I only have one eye. How's that for starters?"

On the first tee of golf courses throughout the world, the question is often asked by someone in a foursome attempting to set the parameters for a match—teaming high and low handicappers together in order to even out the skill levels. Seriously intentioned as the question may be, it often gets a sharp retort, like:

"I've been married now for 20 years."

"Take a good look at me... now, you wonder what my handicap is?"

or...

"Golf!"

What is a handicap, anyway? Webster defines "handicap" as everything from an artificial advantage to a physical disability. What this means is that, as with most of the English-language mysteries of our time, the correct answer is: It all depends.

In the world of golf, a handicap is an advantage given in an effort to equalize a match. In the non-golf world, a handicap is a disadvantage that increases the difficulty of achieving objectives.

To golfers, and to everyone else in the world, handicaps are part of life, and our ability to deal with them effectively is likely to be what determines the level of our success. Handicaps in the world of personal finance may have a profound impact on the judgments we make and ultimately on the way we live our lives.

Handicaps and their impact on the outcome of things, represent just one of the many ways golf seems to be a microcosm of life— its challenges, opportunities, blunders, achievements, victories, losses, and rewards.

And, golf is certainly analogous to investing and wealth management in many ways. The questions we have to deal with on a golf course are, in many instances, the very same ones we encounter when making financial decisions. Do I understand the game? Do I know the course? Before getting started, do I have a plan…and a clear set of objectives? After stopping at the halfway house, is it time to be a little more conservative? How do I recover after hitting a bad shot? What do I have to do to win?

In the pages that follow, we are going to take a look at the many things that golf, financial planning, and (by extension) modern day life have in common. If you're a golfer, the comparisons may very well help to make the game become a little more significant to you. Even if you're not a golfer, they will still help you to reduce your handicap.

So whether you're thinking about golf, wealth management, or any of the other challenges you face in life, it's all about your plan: identifying your goals, time horizon, and risk tolerance, and then developing strategies to achieve your objectives.

When you think about it, it's not just a golf plan, a financial plan, or a family plan. It's a life plan—*your* life plan—and it's up to you what you make of it!

Getting to the green without too much hassle is what it's all about. And, if you can have some fun while doing it, all the better!

Chapter 1

To Begin, Believe in Yourself

"I have to believe in myself. I know what I can do,
what I can achieve."
— SERGIO GARCIA

I didn't start playing golf until I was 48 years old. In my younger life, my buddies and I really enjoyed pickup basketball games, but then the legs start to go, you start pulling muscles, and other age-related physical impediments start to crop up. One day, a friend of mine said, "I'm going to play golf," and a couple of months later I joined him.

So I went out there thinking what a lot of amateur golfers think when they're first starting out. It goes something like this: "I played baseball and this is easy. It's a little white ball just sitting there. No one's trying to hit me or throw anything at me, so how hard can it be?" So you start to play, and you get humbled very quickly.

However, once I started educating myself about golf, often with the help of a professional (see Chapter 3, "Work with a Pro"), I improved—even though I started late, with absolutely no knowledge of the nuances of the game. I believed in myself, and I made something of it.

Even if you've only golfed once or twice (or maybe never) that doesn't mean you can't improve your game and have fun doing it. Likewise, don't assume that financial planning is only for the wealthy. The same concept applies to your financial planning: If you believe in yourself, you can make something of your wealth and security regardless of your current status—but you've got to start now.

Set Realistic Expectations

In both golf and financial planning, you need to believe in yourself, but also set realistic expectations. It's all about your goals, time horizon, and risk tolerance.

If you're starting to play golf and you think you're going to go on tour in the next six months, you may need a wake-up call, as it probably is not going to happen. But if you go out there and you say, "Look, I'm going to have some fun and be with friends, have a couple of laughs, and yes, like most people that have some competitive edge, I do want to improve," then you'll be okay.

In golf, as in financial planning, you might ask yourself, "How much time do I have? How much do I want to practice? How good do I really want to become in this game?" You then set a schedule, because if you think you're just going to go out and play once a week and never practice and never hone your skills, you're probably not going to get that good. And that's okay, if that's your expectation. But if you want to get better, you have to set goals for improving, and then check them off, one by one.

I play golf in a group where the skill levels range from a scratch golfer to a 25 handicap. The 25 handicap may never get better, because he never practices. If I hear one more time from this guy, "Oh crap, do you believe that shot!?" I may lose it. (His shots usually generate a lot of thrashing around in the brush.) Whenever he says that, we're all sitting there going, "Yeah, I believe it, because that's the same shot you make every time."

The reality is that in the beginning, golf is a very frustrating game for most people because of their expectations—and, in my opinion, because it looks so easy. Even pros will make ridiculous shots.

Any challenge can be frustrating, but only if you don't set realistic expectations and plan accordingly—whether you're talking golf, your own financial growth, or life itself. With the right plan, and belief in yourself, you ultimately will find yourself in a better situation.

Chapter 2

Know Your Strengths and Limitations

"I know I am getting better at golf because I am hitting fewer spectators."
— PRESIDENT GERALD R. FORD

G olf is like any other sport in that you need to take a look at yourself. How athletic are you? How flexible are you? If you see people hitting the ball 300 yards, and you're continually hitting it only 190 yards, you have to analyze why.

It could be because of some limitation in your rotation. Or, it could be that you're not strong enough, or perhaps you could use more flexibility. It could be a number of things.

Or, the hard cold reality might be that you're just never going to hit the ball more than 200 yards.

Shooting His Age at 80

I have played with one particular guy who is 80 years old, and yes, he actually shoots his age—in the 80s! He never hits a real long ball, but he is amazingly consistent. He will hit the ball 150 yards, and he has an unbelievable short game. I can't tell you how many times I've heard my golfing partners whisper, "I wish I could play like him."

That guy knows his limitations and works with them.

That's a good thing to think carefully about early on, when you're planning your financial future. You're not going to become a millionaire overnight if you have $10,000, so you have to set expectations that are realistic.

I think the mistake many people make is they try to get rich quick. It's wise to look at your financial planning like a pyramid. When it comes to investments, the base of the pyramid is made up of all of your safe stuff—bank accounts, government bonds, certificates of deposit (CDs), money market investments, cash, etc. This is your foundation.

As you scale up the pyramid, you focus on risk/reward: The higher the potential reward, the higher also the potential loss. At the higher levels, your portfolio may include stocks, bonds, mutual funds, exchange-traded funds (ETFs), large cap, small cap, international markets, developed markets, emerging markets, real estate, commodities, etc.

As you near the top of your investment pyramid, if you have the appetite, you may choose to take even more risk—options, futures, collectibles, and so forth. (I discuss these concepts further in Chapter 13, "Choose the Best Clubs for Each Shot.")

The portfolios of most individuals contain an array of investments, with the bulk somewhere toward the middle of the pyramid, and smaller allocations dedicated to the very top.

There are also some people who actually try to start investing near the top—or rather, they put most of their money, which should be allocated to their foundation and lower-risk asset classes, into those high-risk investments. It seldom works out. Doing that is like building a house of cards: If you have a weak foundation and something happens, everything collapses.

So know your strengths and limitations, and be smart. Like the older guy I play with, don't try to overextend yourself. Be conservative with the bulk of your investments. Take them "150 yards at a time," keeping your goals in sight. You'll still be able to take some additional risk at the right time and in the right situations, but doing it this way will help ensure that you minimize setbacks and maximize your way forward.

To add to the metaphors, musically speaking, don't try to sing like a soprano if you're a baritone. Or, don't buy a two-ton truck if all you need is transportation back and forth to work. Take your best shots for your particular skills and abilities, then use and reuse what works best for you.

Chapter 3

Start with the Basics

*"I started watching golf for the first time yesterday.
I'm really worried about myself. I was actually enjoying it."*
— Ewan McGregor

Every sport has certain fundamentals that everyone adheres to when they start—golf in particular. In golf, you're never going to be any good unless you learn the rules of the game, understand strategy, and practice your technique—the fundamentals. You have to learn how to hold the club, the proper posture, swing mechanics, and body positioning. You have to decide what clubs to buy, and how you may progress in club selection when you get better. You also have to manage your emotions and become resilient, set up step-by-step goals, and plan for the future.

Of course, you also have to learn golf etiquette. Things like: keeping silent on the tee box, never walking across someone's line on the green, and picking up the flag once in a while. Perhaps most of all, golf teaches you the core values of respect, honesty, and perseverance. It builds character and life skills.

Financial planning is the same way. You don't start at the top. You don't get rich overnight. You start with the fundamentals.

Your advisors (lawyers, CPAs, financial advisors, bankers, insurance agents, etc.) should also have the aforementioned core values—respect, honesty, and perseverance.

You Need a Plan

I truly believe that when someone says, "Who needs a financial plan?" the answer is, *everybody*. Yet in the financial process, it's amazing how many people *don't* have that initial plan.

The first question I usually get from clients is, "What is a financial plan?" The answer is simple. It's a snapshot of where you are today (your proficiencies and deficiencies), where you want to be down the road (short- , mid-, and long-term), and what strategies you will develop to get there.

It doesn't matter how much money you have. Financial planning is not one-size-fits-all. Everybody doesn't have the same goal of becoming rich, whatever that means.

Some financial plans are a 50-page document; others can be written on a napkin. Either way, they're all about strategic decisions and a *process*.

The complexity of your financial plan depends on your situation. People with a lot of money often have a lot more moving parts, and may need a lot of aspects of the wealth management process, including portfolio design, tax planning, and risk management, as well as retirement and estate planning.

People with relatively little money, or those just starting out, also need a plan. For them, we create a plan that focuses on accumulating dollars, examining expenses, and managing cash flow.

The interesting thing is that there are a lot of clichés and adages such as, "People don't plan to fail; they fail to plan." But those are so true, because when you speak to people about every other aspect of their lives, whether it's going on vacation or putting an addition on the house, there's always a plan involved.

You don't haphazardly one day wake up and say, "We're going on vacation, what do we pack?" That would be a tough one to answer if you don't know where you're going. You normally have a plan that you're going someplace warm, someplace cold, or to a major city, on a cruise, hiking in the mountains, or whatever. You have a plan.

If you're in the initial stage of financial planning and don't have much money at all, the planning process is all about *how do I accumulate wealth?* The answer could be something as simple as cutting expenses, because at the end of the day there are only two ways you can accumulate money: one is to earn more; the other is to spend less.

Usually it's a combination of both, so people with little money often need help with the cash flow process of the plan. *How do I budget? How do I live within my means?* I delve into this further in Chapter 9, "Minimize Your Expenses."

Risk Management

The basics also include things like risk management. There are four types of risk management: risk acceptance, risk avoidance, risk reduction, and risk transference.

In every single plan, we cover the only three things that can happen to you:

1. You live forever. (Of course, that's not going to happen, but you live to a ripe old age and you're very healthy.)
2. You die prematurely (which means yesterday).
3. An accident or sickness renders you disabled.

Any one of those three things can happen to anyone, so when you put your plan together, you need to do the analytics and ask, "Okay, if I live forever, will I have enough money? If I die prematurely, what will happen to my family? If I can't work anymore, what will happen to me and my family?" You put together the analytics, identify the shortfalls ("here's what can happen"), and then you come up with a remedy. Your risk management plan covers all three contingencies.

In my firm, we like to say to people, "We're going to tell you what's going to happen under each scenario, and you are going to tell us which one you don't want to address. How do you want to prioritize?"

Take insurance, which you can use to hedge against death or disability. I used to think that people hated insurance, including myself. Thirty-five years ago, I figured I didn't need insurance. I was young. I have since come to the conclusion that I don't hate insurance, I just hate *paying for it!*

Everyone I know sees it the exact same way. If I said I could get you $2 million of life insurance for free, you would say, "Sure!" However, when I disclose the premium, many people will make 20 different excuses as to why they shouldn't have it.

It's the same with every kind of risk management, whether it's auto insurance, home insurance, or something else. Some are just necessary evils that you have to have. Personally, I try to have the best affordable coverage available.

Hey…no pain no gain…in golf and in your financial planning!

Chapter 4

Develop Your Strategy

"Competitive golf is played mainly on a five-and-a-half-inch course: the space between your ears."

— BOBBY JONES

If you were to tell me, "I'm a 20 handicap and I'm going to get down to a five," I would probably think, "Lots of luck with that!" But if you say you're a 20 and you want to get down to a 17, I would suggest, "Okay let's talk to a pro and take an assessment." It's like that in financial planning. Where are you today? Where do you want to be down the road? Let's develop a strategy on how to get there.

In financial planning, a strategy is essential. Developing the goal is the first step, and it has to be written. Our practice is to not only develop a financial plan, but also create a written investment policy statement (IPS). This statement defines how much risk you're willing to take, what you want to achieve, and how you want to achieve it.

We look at it every year and consider the following:

1. Did you meet your goal?

2. Are you still the same profile you were a year ago?

3. Do you still want to take the same amount of risk this next year?

I discuss risk and return further in Chapter 12, "Avoid Hazards."

Focusing on Your Goals

To help you reach your goals, we employ strategies such as the following:

- We look at all of your insurance policies, whether you have enough, and whether they are priced optimally for you.

- We develop an investment portfolio that aligns with your risk tolerance, time horizon, and objectives.

- We look at how you are going to retire, how many dollars you will need at that point, and how you are going to get there. How do we coordinate your personal investments with social security and your 401(k)?

- We look at your tax strategy—everything you do with an eye toward reducing what you will owe the government. We look at tax-advantaged investments and your estate plan.

Estate Planning Strategy

Another part of your financial strategy is planning for how to distribute your estate.

Do you have a will? If not, why? If so, then when was the last time it was reviewed? (Things change, you know....marriage, divorce, children...)

Your will is the foundation of your estate plan. Your will states your wishes. You get to name people to make future decisions for you in the event you become incapable of making them on your own. It names executors and guardians, as well as trustees in the event trusts are established.

Upon death, here is how your assets are distributed:

First, they are transferred according to ownership. If you hold anything in joint ownership, specifically joint tenants with rights of survivorship (JTWROS), those assets will pass to the surviving party upon your death.

Second, they are passed by contract. If you have a 401(k), an IRA, life insurance policy, or any other contract naming a beneficiary, that person will receive those assets upon your death. Both of these first two methods of distribution avoid probate.

Third, any remaining assets pass through your will—the document that allows you to define how your possessions are to be distributed, administered, and perhaps managed upon your death. A will can be very simple (thus the term *simple will*), or it can be very complex, involving gifting strategies and trusts with acronyms such as GRATs, GRUTs, CRATs, CRUTs, SLATs, ILITs, etc.

Business owners face even more challenges when dealing with succession planning: How does one develop an exit strategy? Who will take over the business? Are children involved in the business? What about those who are not? Is there a buy/sell agreement in place?

In all of these cases, we start with a very simple process. We'll draw three circles (see the illustration below). Circle one is labeled "Family," circle two is "Charity," and circle three is "IRS." We put a percent sign in each circle and let the client fill it in. What do you think the percentages are? Family is generally in the 90 percent to 100 percent range, but I've never seen anything but zero in the IRS circle.

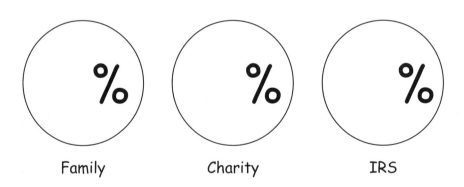

| Family | Charity | IRS |

You may say, "90, 10, 0." We then overlay your exiting plan on the circles, and it may say, "75, 0, 25," and you may say, "Oh gosh, how do I get that IRS down to zero and the charity up to 10?" You put in what you want—you are setting the goals, not me. We just show you how to get there.

Sometimes the simplest things are the best. As I said, it's all about the fundamentals…and in this case the circles are a great visual!

What about You?

Once your estate plan has been established and memorialized, it is extremely important that all of its components are discussed with everyone concerned.

A family discussion of your plan allows everyone to hear and understand your wishes while you are alive, leaving nothing up to interpretation.

We had a situation where a son was disinherited, and the first time he knew about it was when his brother (who was the executor) informed him when the will was read. It was a very uncomfortable situation for all, especially for the executor, who hadn't previously seen the will or been informed of this decision, and had to be the bearer of such news. It was an unfair situation for all, but is easily avoidable.

When it comes to financial planning, don't think only of money. Let the answers to those issues and questions I suggested earlier guide you to a comprehensive "life plan"—one that reflects current and likely future conditions, and is geared to what you and your family want, need, and can realistically hope to achieve.

If you plan well and execute with discipline, that exciting moment when you realize that your goals are within grasp will be much more than a pipe dream. Preparation will meet opportunity, and you'll be in a great position to succeed.

Chapter 5

Work with a Pro

"Golf is deceptively simple and endlessly complicated."
— ARNOLD PALMER

In my experience, there are three types of people who play golf—those who go out and do it on their own, those who get professional help from the get go, and those who try it on their own and quickly (or not so quickly) realize that they need some guidance.

I fall into the last group. When I started playing about 17 years ago, golf looked relatively simple. A little white ball on the ground, and all you had to do is hit it. You could even choose from a variety of different clubs! No one throwing a 90 mph fastball at you, no one trying to block your shot, and no one trying to tackle you....*there is no defense!* As a matter of fact (under the rules of golf etiquette) everyone is required to be silent while you are hitting. *So what can go wrong?*

Let's face it: Plenty of people have walked onto a golf course, having never taken a lesson. A few of them actually have done okay after building up some experience. Many of these same people manage their own finances and some of them are very good at it. Look at Lee Trevino, Ray Floyd, Jim Furyk, and Bubba Watson. They all have unorthodox swings, are self-taught, and have become major champions. I'm not sure if these guys manage their own money, too, but my point is that, although some people can do it on their own and do very well, the vast majority of folks need help with their money and their golf game.

Looking back on my golf experience, I realize that I would have improved much more quickly if I had taken instruction from a golf professional early on.

Like many people, I didn't say, "Let me stop right here and start with a professional." Instead, I told myself, "I can improve on my own." It didn't work out very well, because I just picked up a bunch of bad habits.

Even now, I think sometimes that I have no idea what I'm doing on the golf course. And that's why I still need occasional help. So, I've worked with a pro to improve my game.

In some of my earlier lessons, the pro changed my grip or my stance—things that sound so simple, yet probably would have taken a very long time to figure out on my own.

Or, perhaps I *wouldn't* have figured them out by myself, but the pro was able to point out things that worked because this is what they do for a living. They're able to give you some short-cuts. They look at your physical ability, your mental acuity, how much you really want to put into this game, and the time that you have to practice. Then they set up a program that allows you to improve your game.

In the financial world, the analogy holds. I believe wealth management is part science, part art. Many people try to manage their financial planning on their own, and some are very successful.

However, most people who try to do it on their own miss something. They focus on the obvious, and they usually overlook some important components. So, when you hire a professional financial advisor, that person's job is not to sell you investments or insurance, but rather to assess your situation, look at where you are today and where you want to be at some point down the road, and then develop strategies that will work for you. These strategies take into account both the *quantitative* analysis, based on the size of your estate, and also the *qualitative* analysis, asking: What are your goals? What is your time horizon? What is your risk tolerance? What are the important things in your life? Where do you imagine yourself "down the road?"

I think many people spend much of their time with the quantitative stuff and often neglect the most important question: What do you want out of life?

Sticking with Your Plan

Once you have a financial plan, a pro can help you implement and monitor it. That's very important, because, after all, *imagination without implementation is hallucination!*

Take New Year's Eve resolutions, for example. I may say to my-self, "I'm going to lose 20 pounds this year," but talk is cheap, right? If I don't have an actual plan to do that, by next December I probably will be about 19 pounds away from my goal.

That's because I wasn't consistent, I didn't monitor progress, *and I didn't have somebody to keep me on the program!* When it comes to wealth management, your financial advisor (your "pro") will provide that service and help you to make changes when necessary.

Monitoring is especially critical. How do you know if you're successful if you don't have something to measure it by? People sometime measure their success by generalities, such as, "My portfolio gained 5 percent in the market this year," or, "I'm down 2 percent." That actually may not mean much.

What means more is, "Here was my goal for the year—did I reach it?" The goal might very well be much broader than just gaining that 5 to 10 percent. Perhaps your goal was to save more money, start a college plan for your children, contribute more to your retirement plan, and review your wills and trusts. Did you meet these goals?

Whatever it is, a financial advisor—your pro—very often will help in these areas.

Don't Panic

One of the most important things a financial advisor can do is to keep you from panicking. One of my best golf lessons was with a pro who was very calming. He was a great guy. I would be freaking out with bad shots, and he would say, "relax, take a deep breath." His voice was so soothing. He was able to help reduce my anxiety and help me think positively, which reduced my tension.

Amazingly, I started swinging more easily, and thought, "Oh wow, you're great! You've got to come out with me every day." He kept me from panicking, and it worked.

When all is going well, life is good. But when things get rough—a bad day in the market, for example—people have a tendency to want to jump out of the proverbial window. Most often, they will sell when they're not supposed to sell. Those are the periods when we do the most hand-holding. We can remind people of some historical lessons we have all learned in the market.

So be as good as you can be—both on the golf course and in life. Work with a pro to make sure you reach your goals.

Chapter 6

Get the Right Equipment

"It's about hitting the ball in the center of the
club face and hitting it hard."
— BUBBA WATSON

Years ago, people would buy clubs and play with them for 10 years. I play with Callaway clubs. In recent years, they've come out with the Razr, X Hot, X2Hot, Big Bertha, Great Big Bertha—and the XR16, for which they teamed up with Boeing in order to optimize the club head's aerodynamic efficiency. (It's true, and I know a few guys who swear by it!) The whole high-tech club thing is unbelievable!

To borrow a metaphor from another sport, many of us believe it's the arrows not the archer. We think that a new club is going to make a difference in our game.

I've seen people go to a sporting goods store or online and just buy a club. However, the proper way to get club is to go to a pro, get that person's advice and proceed from there.

I did just that, and the pro gave me five different 7-irons to try. He told me to hit with them. He watched and took notes. When I was finished, he asked me which one I liked the best. When I told him, he then showed me his notes, which confirmed that my preference was in his top two. He then asked me something I thought was strange at first: Which club did I think *looked* the best? He said it was important for the club to not only feel right but look right to you as well.

That's important. Your comfort level is determined by not only how a club feels in your hands, and how well you can hit with it, but how you feel emotionally when you put it down to look at it. (I suppose this psychology is similar to "dress for success" or "look good, feel good!") The pro will assist you, and after you hit a bunch of shots, he'll advise you on which clubs would be the best for you.

Then, if you really want to take it to the next level, you can get fitted. Clubs are designed for people of different heights, weights, body types and so forth, so someone who knows what they're doing can fit you and give you a custom feel.

Equipment Is Product

In financial planning, we look at the financial products that will help you get to where you want to be as your "equipment." In other words, we are going to examine investment choices, consider whether they will do what they are intended to do, and whether they look and feel right to you. If you are ever uncomfortable with an investment, get rid of it (just like your clubs).

Just as there are clubs for short distance, long distance, sand, and rough, there are specialized investments for short term, long term, safe, speculative, growth, income, and so forth.

There are a plethora of investment choices. What's important is picking the right ones for you—the ones that you are most comfortable with.

And just as testing helps you pick the right clubs, planning helps you determine the right investments choices.

First, we'll customize your plan and then we'll go out and find the right products for you. As with golf, you may want to have the latest and greatest. Should you buy commodities, options, oil and gas? For most people, a basic portfolio consists of traditional stocks and bonds, treasuries, real estate, and so forth. If you have enough money and want to climb up the risk ladder a little bit, then you may want to explore some of that other "more exotic" stuff.

Leverage All of Your Tools

Once you start playing, take advantage of the 14 clubs that are in your bag. Every club has unique capabilities, and you need to understand what each one can do for you.

For example, for the longest time, if I had a chip shot or a similar shot of about 40 yards to the green, I went to my 56-degree wedge every single time. But over the last couple of years, I learned that I could use an 8-iron or 7-iron and generally do different things, like "bump and run" with my clubs. So take advantage of what your other clubs can do to change your whole game. (I discuss this further in Chapter 13, "Select the Best Club for Each Shot.")

So, you have to look at everything you have—all of the equipment that's available. I make sure that mine is better than average, and sometimes that's where the professional comes in. Also, you may have certain knowledge about what's available for you, but not the whole picture, and that's another area where a professional can help you by making suggestions, limiting risk, and improving your game. Of course, it's the same with financial planning. (See Chapter 5, "Work with a Pro," for more of my thoughts about this.)

Finding the Right Fit

Having the knowledge to know what fits where is critical. If you are someone who needs income, you should create a strategy in order to achieve a certain annual yield. So, you go out and hunt the product world. You might look at the bond and real estate markets, dividend stocks, or master limited partnership (MLPs)—all different vehicles that can produce income. With the help of a pro, you come up with a plan that can give you that yield at an accepted risk.

So, getting the right equipment for financial planning is not about looking at the shiny object, it's all about the fit.

Most of the time I play with Titlist ProV1 golf balls. One of the reasons I do is because that's the ball used by many of the pros (I heard that in a commercial). The ProVs cost more than many of the other brands, and at my level I'm not sure a less expensive ball would hurt my game much.

But I'm not going broke buying them, and I don't want any excuses (balls, clubs, etc.) for a bad round, so I suppose I'll continue to support Titleist.

A lot of us think that the *most expensive product* is what we need, and the reality is that's not always true. It's the same in financial planning and investments. When we recommend investments for our portfolios, there is a considerable amount of time that goes into the analytics, and costs are always a consideration.

There are a million commercials selling equipment. There is no shortage of guys on TV at night telling us to put gold in our IRA or buy real estate with no money down.

There are loads of magazines telling us of last year's top 10 best investments, not to mention those newsletters that claim they could teach us how to get a triple-digit return on our money! Frankly, I think we're bombarded with too much of this stuff.

When it comes to your financial planning, don't get blinded by the glare of shiny objects, as they may not necessarily be the right fit for your current situation and goals. Get the "equipment" that fits and will really work for you.

Chapter 7

Practice Early and Often

"It's a funny thing: The more I practice, the luckier I get."
— ARNOLD PALMER

In golf, practice is very important. Heck, in every sport you ever played as a kid—basketball, baseball, football, whatever—I'll bet you practiced 75 percent of the time and played the game the other 25 percent of the time.

It's not necessarily that way in golf, but it should be. Many people I know (including myself) hardly ever get out to the range, and those who are more dedicated still don't get out as much as they play. One of the reasons for this is that golf is a very time-consuming sport. If you get into a pick-up basketball game, you're finished in an hour. If you go to play golf, it can take four hours or more, and that's without the hamburger and beer. And it's expensive!

All of this dissuades people from practicing a lot, me included. If I have time, I'd rather play.

The better golfers I play with definitely spend more time practicing. They go to the range once or twice a week. They take a
lesson now and then. I know this scratch golfer, and he still takes
lessons. I'm thinking, "Holy smokes, this guy's commitment to
golf is certainly a lot greater than mine!" It's no wonder he plays
so well.

Developing "Feel"

Being good at golf is very much about "feel." I can't tell you
how many times I've played a 390- or 410-yard hole and gotten
20 yards from the green in two shots. Two shots! And I wind
up getting a six. (Have you ever "skulled" or "chunked" a shot?
Not to mention the dreaded "shank-a-pot-o-mus?")

In these cases I was in great shape, but I blew it on my next
shots. Being consistently good at these kinds of things comes
from practice. The guys who perform really well know exactly
what shot they want to hit, and they don't limit themselves.

That comes from practice and experience, and it comes with
knowledge. It's the same thing in the financial world. You
have to know what your expectations are, what you're trying
to achieve, and what you need to do to make those dreams and
goals come true.

Develop Your Cadence

Rushing into anything is much more likely to be foolish than
smart, so why tread on unsafe ground? That's true for golfers

running out to the first tee, where the rush is likely to cause a dubbed drive, from which recovery will take three or four holes *if you're fortunate!*

Guess what? You see this same dynamic with investors who are frantically tossing hard-earned money after a hot tip, or guessing that a big market turn is going to happen before lunch time.

Now imagine this: A few days ago, your buddy gave you a nudge and a wink when the TV report said "XYZ" stock has gone up 10 points. He said, "Boy, you'd better get on that one! I've heard it's about to take off." Your buddy's a pretty smart guy, so you borrow some money from your kid's college fund and put it all on XYZ. A week later, your buddy is patting himself on the back for having escaped before XYZ slid down the slippery slope by 30 points...with you on board. Effectively, you've reached out to the financial world's first tee, and dubbed your drive.

In this case, all of that relaxing and practicing that has served you so well on the golf course got lost in the anxiety of cashing in quick. You hadn't yet developed a "cadence" in your financial life.

Cadence in finance is very much like the practice swing in golf. It's the procedure you use that's helped to develop a winning way. You select your club based on a review of what the distance is, and what works for you at that distance. You consider the likelihood of whether that club is going to get you over the trap in front of the green, and if the risk is worth it. Should you go for it, or lay it up? How about the wind? Where is your opponent? Will you still be in the hole if you don't hit the shot or if it goes in the ditch? Where does the match stand? Can you afford to lose the hole?

Bit by bit, you've been gathering and processing that data on your way to your ball. You don't wait until you get there to start. If you do, you lose that all-important cadence, and you'll also hold up play. Taking each shot is a *process*—it includes several stages—some mental and some physical—that happen in sequence and in rhythm. By practicing that process over and over—developing your cadence—you'll learn what works, and what you need to make each shot a success.

Get Educated

Practice in wealth management really means getting educated. It means learning about financial planning in general, learning about investments, insurance, and your 401(k) plan, and becoming fairly knowledgeable in all of those areas. You don't have to be an expert in them, but you should at least know the jargon so that you can have an intelligent conversation with someone.

With financial planning, the practice part is developing your cadence and reading up—maybe watching some of those financial shows once in a while (and taking their advice with a little skeptical analysis), and maybe reading a periodical—again, learning the fundamentals.

Success in golf requires keeping your head down. Success in financial planning means keeping "heads up." Each takes discipline. How do you improve your discipline? Plenty of practice!

Chapter 8

Work on Your Short *and* Long Game

"It's good sportsmanship to not pick up lost golf balls
while they are still rolling."
— MARK TWAIN

If you're an average golfer, you want to hit the ball 250 yards. Of course, you're going to try to do that with your driver, not a 9-iron, because it is most definitely not going to happen with the latter.

The same thing holds true if you want to chip onto the green and you're 40 yards away. You're not going to use your driver, but rather a club that can effectively send your ball that smaller distance with accuracy. Or, if you're facing a long fairway that doglegs around a clump of trees before reaching the green, you'd be smart not to try hitting the ball over those woods. It would be smarter to take a couple of shorter shots to get you there with more certainty. You could call that your short game strategy.

Financial planning is very similar, because you know that if you need money a year from now to buy a home (your "short game" goal), you will need to have "x" amount of dollars saved at that point, and it will *have* to be there—liquid and ready to use. In such a case, you can't take a chance with a long-term investment—one that may provide a good return over the next 10 or 20 years, but with expected volatility in-between.

We just don't know what a long-term investment will be worth in the next six months to a year. However, we can project an estimated future value over a 10-year period based on historical data.

Consider this: If my kid was going to college in two months, it would be silly for me to take that college money and put it in the stock market. For the short term, that is just too unpredictable. With this type of goal, our advice would be to find an ultra-short-term, safe investment that has zero loss of principal—for example, short-term CDs, money markets, or treasuries.

The cost of this will be a very low return, but the benefit will be that the money will be there in two months to pay tuition.

This is the difference between a return on capital and a return of capital.

Covering Both "Short" and "Long"

It's critical to pay attention to both your long and short game in golf. In financial planning it's the same. You have to know what's out there, define your expectations, and be satisfied with your decision.

Here's the trade-off: In the very short term (that college tuition, for example), you can't afford to lose one penny. That is going to limit the types of investments you can make, and you're not going to get that much return either. Your sacrifice is you're going to make a lot less than you could potentially make somewhere else, but you're going to have your principal when you need it.

Conversely, long-term goals allow you to seek capital appreciation over time, thus opening up the world of investment choices and opportunities.

A typical long-term goal is retirement. For most of us, our retirement income will come from three sources: Social Security, retirement plans, and personal savings and investments.

In the near term, Social Security benefits will likely be available for all of us. Down the road…who knows? The key is to manage how and when you take Social Security in order to maximize the money that eventually (hopefully) will come your way. Remember, Social Security is not an entitlement program—we've paid into it throughout all of our working years!

Retirement plans—pensions, profit sharing, 401(k)s, 403(b)s, IRAs, defined benefit plans, cash balance plans, and others—will play a big part in most individuals' quality of life after their working years. You should take full advantage of these plans—for example, maximizing your contributions in your 401(k) in order to accumulate the most you can for retirement.

Keep in mind that all retirement income (from profit sharing, 401(k)s, 403(b)s, IRAs, etc.) that has been growing tax-deferred will be fully taxable as ordinary income at time of distribution. For that reason, many people do not take their distribution until they are forced to due to the required minimum distribution (RMD) at age 70½.

In the meantime it's usually more tax effective to receive income from your individual investments.

No matter where your income is going to come from, it is clear that if your goal is to have a "comfortable retirement," you need to first define "comfortable," and then you need to put a plan in place to get there.

In golf, the average person very often loves to try to smash the ball and get a long drive. But sometimes the results are less than stellar, and in reality that often doesn't serve your best interest.

Think of that older guy I know who hits the ball just 150 yards—again, and again…and again. Also think of a guy like Bubba Watson, who can drive the ball a mile, but would never have won any of those tournaments without skillful chips and putts (skills that seem better on some days than others).

The Bottom Line

In golf, financial planning, and life itself, you've got to be conservative sometimes, mixing your long-term strategies with those short-term "sure things."

We can't live in the short term. There is too much noise for that. If the Dow is down 100 points and everybody freaks out, well guess what? That's a short-term problem. If you have a long-term plan, you should be comfortably equipped to ride out those short-term incidents. They shouldn't affect the long-term plan in general.

Our philosophy is to live life today and be confident about tomorrow!

In golf, if you hit a bad shot, it doesn't mean your round is over. It simply means you hit a bad shot, period. You need to get it out of your head and move forward.

Bobby Jones famously said that golf is played in the five-and-a-half inches between your ears. Sometimes we bog down our minds with so many different things that we get away from the basics. Just think about that.

Chapter 9

Minimize Your Expenses

"A man who both spends and saves money is the happiest man, because he has both enjoyments."
— SAMUEL JOHNSON

Most average golfers think that "it's the arrows not the archer." In other words, they believe that laying down some big bucks on the latest, greatest equipment is going to change their life.

We all go out and buy the latest stuff, and at the end of the day, $300 for a single club doesn't seem like a lot until you go in your basement and find a bag full of $300 clubs, and you think, "Oh my gosh, I spent all this money and my game didn't improve."

The point here is that you have to watch your expenses because you can find yourself spending a heck of a lot of money in this game and not improving.

Maybe it's not so much the amount of money you're spending, but the direction in which you're spending it! Think about this: What is the amount of money you spend on clubs, clothes, shoes, etc., versus lessons and practice? Which will help you improve more?

Of course, equipment is important, but again, it's usually not the arrows, but the archer who makes the difference.

Managing Your Cash Flow

In financial planning, one of the processes we go through is *cash flow analysis:* money coming in and money going out. We actually don't like to use the word "budget," because people freak out. Nobody likes to be on a budget, but a cash flow plan (sounds better, doesn't it?) is important, so that you know what you're living with.

There are only a couple of ways to get a handle on expenses in order to accumulate more money. It's really very simple: You can earn more, spend less, or embark on a combination of the two.

Unfortunately, people who have nine-to-five jobs get a salary and that's it; the opportunities to earn more can be somewhat limited. For them, spending less is especially critical.

If you ask people, "How much do you make?" 90 percent of them will know the answer. They have a pretty good handle on what comes in, especially those folks who are on straight salary. They know that they make, for instance, $80,000 a year. It's a simple given.

If you ask people how much they *spend,* 90 percent of them know the cost of five or six big-ticket items—the car payment, the mortgage, their last vacation. However, very often they may wonder, "Well, where did the rest of the money go?"

At the end of the day, if you ever want to accumulate wealth, if you make $100 and spend $100, you have a problem. If you make $100 and only spend $80 (after taxes and everything else), but you can't identify the other $20, you still have a problem.

So, getting a handle on expenses is critical.

Often times, when someone cannot identify where the discretionary money is, we will fine-tune their recollection of expenses. We'll go through the expenses again. Usually they're leaving something out—perhaps the extra hundred bucks they put in their wallet every week, which seems to disappear into a black hole.

We've all heard the stories about buying one less Starbucks per day over the course of the year and saving something like $2,000. That small stuff adds up!

The Joy of Compounding

Here's a tip: If you start to save sooner, you don't have to take as much from your pocket. That's due to compounding. Consider this: Somebody getting into the workforce in his 20s can put away $3,000 to $4,000 a year and end up with a significant nest egg ($3,000 x 40 years with 5 percent interest= $362,000). If you start in your 40s or 50s, however, you would have to put away $10,000, $12,000 or more annually just to end up with the same amount at age 65 as the guy who started saving at 25.

So the sooner you start, the better it is, because you have a couple of things working for you: the money going in for a longer period of time, and the compounding, which is fantastic. It's interest on top of interest, and you would be surprised at how much people can accumulate!

How many people, for example, wonder how they're going to pay for their kids' college when it's already too late to save? If they start when the child is two—instead of 17—and put money away every year, they could quite possibly have the full tuition and even retirement money 20 years later.

I read that when Albert Einstein was asked to name the greatest invention in human history, he replied, "compound interest."

I think I've made my point!

Chapter 10

Keep Your Eye
on the Ball

*"When I'm in a zone, I don't think about the
shot or the wind or the distance or the gallery or anything;
I just pull a club and swing."*
— MARK CALCAVECCHIA

A nybody who is good at golf—whether it's a golf pro giving you a lesson, or a friend trying to school you in the intricacies and pleasures of the game—will tell you to keep your head down when you're swinging to strike the ball.

There's a reason for that: If you take your eye off the ball when the club hits it, usually bad things happen. You tend to open or close the face of the club, which can cause a slice or a hook, or you could even execute the dreaded chunk or skull shot!

Your swing and your rhythm are thrown off, and your balance is skewed during your follow-through.

Here's something that's especially interesting: The skill of keeping your eye on the ball runs contrary to the skills needed in most other sports you have ever played. For example, when you throw a football, your eye is on the target, not the ball. It's the same with basketball—your eye is on the target!

This may be why it is difficult for some of us who did not grow up playing golf to break the habit of looking up at the target.

So while you're doing all of that practicing in the hope of improving your game, you really should follow this simple advice: Keep your eye on the ball!

In the financial realm, that means keeping your focus on the ongoing performance of your financial tools and strategies, whether you're saving for college, building up a nest egg for retirement, or just reaching a certain level of comfort.

Keeping your eye on the ball also means staying the course, even in bad times, in order to get to the good times. In financial terms, that means not panicking—for example making a rash decision because the market went down 200 points one day. Believe me, the majority of times, that kind of fear-based decision will come back to bite you, and when you look back on the incident, you will most definitely be sorry that you let up on your focus in that most critical juncture.

Many years ago, I went to a baseball seminar with major league Hall of Famer Ted Williams, one of the greatest hitters of all time. He gave a talk and said that when he played *he actually saw the moment the ball hit the bat.* Now that's incredible! Talk about focus, discipline, and keeping your eye on the ball!

It Takes Discipline

Keeping your eye on the ball is also about discipline. Yes, staying disciplined can be challenging in many situations, but I urge you to think about this statement, which I've repeated to many people, including my kids:

What is worse: the pain of discipline or the pain of regret?

I believe that the pain of discipline is not that bad compared to the pain of regret, because with the latter, there's nothing you can do about it.

In dealing with your financial life, it takes discipline to save money, to live within your means, to curb your debt, to contribute the max to your 401(k), to start and maintain a college fund for the kids, or any number of other actions.

What if you don't do these things? What are the consequences? How bad is the pain of regret?

It is critical to set realistic goals and expectations. These should be written so that you can periodically refer back to them to see if you are on target. Focusing on these things amounts to keeping your eye on the ball.

In every aspect of life, doing the same thing over and over again and expecting different results is the quintessential definition of insanity. As you execute your financial strategy, there will be times when things don't work out as expected and you hit a "bad shot." The key will be to not lose focus and stay in the game. You may have done something that you can correct yourself, or you may need someone to look things over in order to help you get back on track. Either way, the key is to recognize that you may be off course, and figure out a way to adjust your "swing."

That, too, is keeping your eye on the ball, and it is an essential practice for achieving your success.

Chapter 11

Work on Your Follow-Through

"Swing easy and hit hard."

— Julius Boros

I n golf, the physical act of follow-through is easy to under-stand. Take aim, get in your stance, grip your club proper-ly, take your club back, and swing with timing and tempo, continuing the motion so that you have a smooth momentum as the club passes through the ball like a pendulum.

That's the ideal, but actually executing good follow-through is harder than it looks. For a lot of people, the follow-through doesn't look like the ideal at all, but like a rough and jerky chop. Either they don't take their club back far enough, or they don't smoothly swing through the ball and continue the motion.

Getting this right is difficult for most people. Generally you don't have a camera recording your swings, and you don't practice in front of a mirror. If you can't observe yourself, it's tougher to improve. A coach or friend can try to point out what you're doing wrong, and provide some techniques with which you can practice. If you really stick to it, you will usually improve.

I've seen that first hand. But beware—there is certainly no shortage of well-meaning people willing to give you "tips." Take advice from people you trust—those who, you believe, know what they're doing.

The Stroke and the Follow-Through

In golf, the stroke is defined as the forward movement of the club made with the intention of striking and moving the ball forward.

In financial planning, the follow-through is the *implementation* of your financial plan. That is truly where the "club strikes the ball."

Someone once said: "Imagination without implementation is hallucination." That is so true. If you imagine something, and you have a concrete idea of what you want to do, but you don't follow through and implement it, it's never going to happen.

So, the first concept in following through with regard to financial planning is simply doing what you plan to do. We tell every client to *never* do anything they're not entirely comfortable with. If we didn't explain a concept or strategy properly, or if our client is, for any reason, having a difficult time understanding it, then we say, "Let's take a step back until you're ready."

If you don't fully understand something, don't do it. Get to the bottom of the concept. Learn it backwards and forwards, developing your grasp of all of the ways it can play out, as well as the risks involved. Then, when you are ready, *take the club back and swing.* That's implementation!

Follow-Through = Adjustments

There is even more to the concept of follow-through. It's also about your financial plan itself, which is not the paper or the book in which it is written, but the ongoing relationship between you, your plan, and the ever-changing landscape.

The planning process is dynamic. Financial conditions on the macro level are going to change every single day. Some aspects of the economic landscape you can control, some you can't. You therefore need to review your plan periodically so that you can analyze what's working and what's not. Are you achieving your goals, or falling short? Is it the fault of the particular investment, or just a macro-economic dip that you should ride out?

Then you adjust by fine-tuning your plan for the future in order to stay on track with your goals. That, too, is follow-through.

We hold monthly investment committee meetings where we analyze portfolios in order to decide, among other things, whether or not performance is due to market conditions, or decisions made by the various investment managers. On occasion, if an investment is not performing up to expectations, we analyze these factors. If the sub-par performance is due to decision making, we put the managers involved on a "watch list," and if they remain on that list for a specified period of time, they are replaced. However, in many instances, performance may be tied to the overall market. In that case, the manager wouldn't necessarily get a pink slip.

Practicing your follow-through in all of its aspects—whether with golf or in the world of financial planning and investing—will help assure your successful progress down the course.

Chapter 12

Avoid Hazards

"There is an old saying: If a man comes home with
sand in his cuffs and cockleburs in his pants,
don't ask him what he shot."
— SAM SNEAD

Just like planning for how you will handle a course's bunkers, water hazards, sloped greens, and fiendish doglegs, you need to also evaluate your investment risks.

On the golf course, hazards are risky indeed. Based on your skill and experience, you have to really think about how you're playing on any particular day, and what kind of risk you are willing to take to get over that trap or pond.

Let's say that you have a 210-yard shot to make it over the water, and you're just not feeling it that day. Maybe you want to lay up so that you have your most comfortable "go-to" shot to the green in three, thus reducing the probability of putting one in the drink.

On another day, when you're feeling better about your performance, you might want to take that shot—and assume that risk. You will feel comfortable about picking the right club and taking a good swing. Knowing your skills and ability on that day, you will feel reasonably comfortable that the risk will pay off for you.

That's essentially what's involved when you're playing around hazards as well. In golf, the risk/reward analysis often comes into play, and there is definitely a correlation between those analytics and your "golf IQ."

Risk vs. Return

In the world of financial planning, the rule of thumb is that the more you risk, the better the potential return should be.

Investments that have a higher potential rate of return usually have a higher risk of losing the principal that you invested. Investments with an anticipated lower rate of return usually have a lower risk of losing principal. This is called a risk/return trade-off.

Since no one knows the future, you cannot be 100-percent sure any investment will do well. Remember the commercial: Past performance is no guarantee of future results.

One of the basic risk-management strategies is diversification. If you diversify your investments with different asset classes and time horizons, one of them can go sour without severe impact to your overall portfolio. You can hit one bad shot without ruining your whole game.

Controlling Your Financial Hazards

Financially we have all different kinds of hazards—some that we can control, and some that we can't due to the economic environment. For example, the price of oil, interest rates, and geopolitical situations are hazards that have a cause and effect on everything that we do. We need to assess them, and then come up with your personal risk assessment: How much risk are *YOU* willing to take to accomplish your goal?

Here's an exercise that we very often do with clients. We might ask, "What's more important to you—not making as much, or not losing as much?" Many people are willing to take less participation on the upside as long as they also take less participation on the downside. Even though it's almost impossible to prevent any loss in a downward market, it is much easier to rebound from coming off of higher lows. Again, it all boils down to the amount of risk you are willing to take.

Once people understand that concept, they not only choose their investments more carefully, but also begin to understand how to define and manage their expectations.

As discussed in Chapter 3, "Start with the Basics," once you define your risk, you can either accept it, or you can employ ways to avoid, reduce, or transfer it. For example, how do you want to financially protect yourself when driving a car? Do you just want to accept the risk of something happening? Or, do you want to stop driving so that you avoid the risk completely?

You can reduce the risk by driving more carefully (no phoning, texting, or applying makeup). You also can *transfer* the risk to an insurance carrier, which, in the event that something does happen, would allow your insurance policy to mitigate your financial loss.

This example is not that different in the world of wealth management, where we assess risk every day from an insurance perspective. What if you die or become disabled? What if you get sick? What if you need long-term care? There is a probability of that happening, so how much risk do you want to keep on your own plate, or how much do you want to transfer to someone else?

I can tell you this: I have never complained at the end of the year that I didn't get to use my homeowners or auto insurance policies. To take that a step further, I have never complained about not using my health insurance, disability, long-term care, or life insurance policies (although the last one would be difficult, since I wouldn't be here to complain).

But I think you get the point. I certainly do raise an eyebrow when the premiums come due, but at that point I have assessed the risk/reward and determined the value of my decision.

These are all factors which need to be carefully considered when you evaluate the hazards that lie before you in your financial planning. As with the hazards on the golf course, they are all manageable—you just need to make intelligent trade-offs.

Chapter 13

Select the Best Club for Each Shot

"Give me golf clubs, fresh air and a beautiful partner, and you can keep the clubs and the fresh air."
— JACK BENNY

D iversification is extremely valuable. In golf you are allowed to carry 14 clubs in your bag. Do you have 14 drivers? How about 14 putters? You may carry several wedges, but certainly not 14 of them! Why? Because that would be ridiculous. You need certain clubs to do certain things.

Nobody carries two of the exact same club. There is a very good reason for that.

However, a golfer might carry some variations on the same club. I see a lot of people, myself included, who have a couple different kinds of wedges. One may be a 60-degree version; the other may be a 56-degree model. You could use one for getting out of a sand trap, while the other might be perfect for clearing a water hazard.

So, you might have a couple of wedges at the most. Nobody carries two drivers, and I've never met anyone that carried two 9 irons!

Also consider this: In golf you use the driver 14 to 15 times per round, at most. You certainly don't use it on the par 3s. However you may use your putter an average of 36 times in each round! (I've known some people to use it even more often!) That being said, when people go to the range, what club do they like to hit the most?

I've seen people spend an inordinate amount of practice time with the clubs they use the least. That doesn't seem to make sense. Remember golf IQ! You've got to be smart about these things.

Diversify to Succeed

Just like the clubs in your bag, diversification is also important to financial planning. You should not fill your financial golf bag with drivers alone, so to speak. In other words, your portfolio should not consist of only long-term investments, or only short-term investments, for that matter.

Your portfolio should include an emergency fund—readily accessible liquid assets that have very little to no probability of losing principal. The usual recommendation is that these funds cover at least three to six months of living expenses.

Just as in golf, where there are long clubs for long distance and shorter clubs for short shots, your portfolio should be designed to meet all of your goals, whether they are short or long. And just like in golf, you do not want to use your long-term investments to meet short-term goals. You do not use your driver to putt! (See Chapter 8, "Work on Your Short and Long Game," for more of my thoughts on this.)

Another reason for diversification is that markets are cyclical, and usually when something is going up, something else is probably going down, or vice versa. The problem we have is detecting when and how the markets are going to react before they do.

So unless you have a very high tolerance for risk, and you're willing to subject your entire portfolio to going in any one direction at any one time, you should diversify. Portfolio diversification allows you to participate in various segments of both the equity and fixed-income markets. Although this decreases the probability of the entire portfolio going up at the same time, it also lessens the risk of it all going *down* at the same time.

If you had kept all of your financial eggs in an S&P 500 index fund in 2008, you would have lost approximately 40 percent of your portfolio. However, with a mix of stocks, bonds, real estate, and other asset classes, you may have been down around 25 percent. Although a 25 percent loss is not good, compare it to the alternative. It allows you to recover faster by "rebounding from higher lows." Keep in mind that if you were invested and didn't get out before the crash, there was really no escape unless you were 100 percent in cash or treasuries (hindsight is 20/20).

Twenty-five percent versus 40 percent? I'll take that deal any day. Remember—*coming off of higher lows.*

Here's another thing that not everybody understands: If you lose 50 percent of your portfolio, some may think that you have to come back 50 percent to get even, but the reality is that you have to come back 100 percent. If you've got $100 and you're down $50, you've got to make $50, which is 100 percent of what you had.

You want to mitigate some of that downside, so diversify! Don't carry a bag full of drivers!

Chapter 14

Remain Flexible

"My father had a lot of compassion about things in life. There were rules, but there also was flexibility within those rules."

— TOM WATSON

There's no doubt that the more flexible you are with your golf swing, the more torque you tend to create, and the longer shots you'll hit. With investing, it's the same thing. You need to have some flexibility as you experience the unexpected economic and social forces in order to attempt to buffer the markets. In the financial world, we are often subjected to what is commonly called "headwinds."

As in golf, you need to learn the shots necessary to play in all types of conditions. Both bull and bear markets offer certain challenges and opportunities.

Physical Flexibility

In golf, you need both physical and mental flexibility. Take a look at some of these golf pros that look like they don't even shave yet. Heck, they look like they're 120 pounds soaking wet, yet they hit these great, long shots off the tee. You stare at them and you wonder, "How can I hit a ball like they do?"

You don't even need a pro for a role model. Once when I was in Florida, I went down to the golf course one day and saw this girl on the driving range with her mom and instructor. She had to be no more than 10 years old, yet I had never seen a more perfect golf swing in my life.

Probably because of her age, she just had all of this flexibility. Her swing was *perfect*, and I just stood there thinking to myself that I would do anything for that swing.

Having physical flexibility is paramount for doing well in golf, but you have to manage your expectations. At least, I do. That's because at my age, I know that I can wish all I want, but I'm not going to have that kid's flexibility.

So the next question is: How much flexibility can you get? And what can you do with that flexibility to improve your game? You can't pretend that you're 20 years old again. Our bodies change, and you have to manage different aches, pains, and all of that other bothersome stuff that is largely out of your control.

If you can't achieve the maximum physical flexibility, what can you do to compensate? In order to hit clean, crisp iron shots, you need to be able to come fully through the ball. As we get older, our knees and hips don't always cooperate with our desire to "swing through." Sometimes, something as simple as opening your front foot may allow for your hips to rotate a little easier.

Maybe you want to go to the range and practice various techniques, or maybe take a few lessons and have someone give you some instruction that can help.

Mental Flexibility

Mental flexibility works in somewhat the same way. There is a line that goes, "I've already made up my mind, don't confuse me with the facts." We all know that person, who, no matter what you tell them, is dead-set on what they believe, what shot they're going to take, or who they're voting for. In golf, financial planning, politics, and every other part of our lives, there are people who have just made up their minds, regardless of the facts.

I'm not perfect, but I try to improve every day in being as open-minded as I can be. In politics, for example: I lean a little to the right, but I'm not too far right. I love talking to people on the left, because I want to learn what I'm missing. I go into every conversation thinking, if they can change my mind, it would be good, because it's healthy to be open-minded.

For the record, I do not think that either side has a corner on the market for all the good ideas, or the bad ones for that matter. And although I consider myself to be open-minded, my belief system has not changed much over the years.

In golf, mental flexibility is often about understanding what you can do to advance the ball and get it to the hole. There is no use dwelling on past bad shots—you have to keep a clear head. Remember, the most important shot you are going to take is the one you're taking now.

For example, your ball is against the opposite side of a tree, and there's no way you can hit it in any kind of a proper way. You may take your club, turn it around, and hit a "lefty shot" just to get away from that damn tree trunk, or hit it between your legs, or something else that's crazy just to get the ball out of there. Or, you may take an "unplayable," take the penalty, and play for bogie (vs. double or triple bogie)!

With most things, I want to be flexible, and that includes investing. In that area, too, I don't want to be the person who says, "I've already made up my mind so don't confuse me with the facts." As in golf and life, you need to have some flexibility in investing.

Any market-based investment is going to go through some bad lies. If an investment doesn't turn out as envisioned at the onset, what do you do?

Although it may be difficult to know when to buy, sometimes it's often more difficult to know when to sell. Being "married" to an investment, holding on forever (sometimes due to emotional reasons), or selling prematurely are common mistakes investors make, and each has its own consequences.

I often say that there are the two "Es" of investing—the economic and the emotional. Each one is critically important. You must recognize which one is influencing your decisions, and why.

It's important to remain flexible and adjust when necessary. Evaluate the current landscape, adjust your follow-through, and get some torque going! (You can read more about this in Chapter 11, "Work on Your Follow-Through.")

With a little of that kind of flexibility, combined with some counseling from a pro, you will hopefully achieve your intended results regardless of the external forces that are trying to throw you off.

Chapter 15

Stay Patient

"A good golfer has the determination to win and the
patience to wait for the breaks."
— GARY PLAYER

I n golf, you need patience. Everybody is going to hit a bad
shot. I watched a tournament recently and even the pros
were hitting balls in the water. I'm thinking *holy cow*, these
guys are professionals, and look at them!

I've played with guys who curse and throw clubs. I even saw a
guy break a club over his knee. To begin, that's very unprofes-
sional. Furthermore, he just lost a club that he'll have to replace,
so it's a pretty stupid action on his part. But emotions sometimes
take over.

You need to remember that the end game is to finish all 18 holes
with the best score you can. You cannot let a couple of bad shots
throw off your whole game.

If you're going to be successful in golf, you need to have patience. You could have an absolutely terrible and embarrassing shot, but the pros teach you that once that happens, you need to forget about it. It's over. Done.

They then remind you that the most important shot in golf is the one you're taking now.

Staying the Course

In financial planning, the phrase is, "stay the course" and wait for your investment benefits to accrue. In the previous chapter I write about flexibility—the ability to change things up when needed. Of course, that is very important. At times you need to make some changes in your investment strategy and portfolio in response to performance issues—whether they are caused by internal or external factors. However, you also need to be patient!

Most people who make money do not do so overnight. They make money over a long period of time

Warren Buffett, the CEO and largest shareholder of Berkshire Hathaway, is considered to be one of the most successful investors in the world. Everyone watches his market moves and studies his every pronouncement. On numerous occasions he has said something along the lines of, "Over the long run, you always make money in the stock market."

That's a great line because the key phrase is *over the long run.* The problem for many folks is when stocks go down, they tend to panic and sell. What creatures of habit we are! We know from past experience that when the stock market goes down, it doesn't stay down. It has bounced back up every time, without exception, and in the past year or so has attained the largest valuation in history. Now keep in mind I am talking about the stock market in general—not any one specific stock. Of course, any one stock *could* take a tumble and never recover.

But when the market goes down, how many people run out and buy, snapping up those bargains? Not many. As a matter of fact, the first inclination of many is to sell.

Let's say that there's a store with a sign in the window that says, "Everything 20 percent off!" How many people will run in to snatch up some bargains? Plenty! You know why?

"This Time It's Different"

Sir John Templeton, another famous investor and mutual fund pioneer, once said that the four most dangerous words in investing are: "This time it's different." Think about that. Every time something bad happens, such as the stock market dropping hundreds of points, they say, "I know it has come back in the past, *but this time it's different.*"

Between wars, presidential assassinations, oil embargos, recessions, and terrorist attacks like 9/11, we have been through some horrible things, and yet it seems that we are always able to "bounce back." Yet the next time a horrible thing happens, somebody is going to say, "Yeah, but this time is different." This mindset may cause you to make some rash emotional decisions, and if we look back (although it is not our intent to profit from tragedies), one would have been better off staying put or maybe even buying at the lows.

The takeaway is this: Even with the best past-performance data, you can't predict what the market is going to do day-by-day or month-by-month. Even the pros on Wall Street don't always make money with day trading—despite the split-second transactions and market-moving deals they have at their disposal. The most successful investors know that the key to wealth accumulation is having a long-term view— remaining patient.

Chapter 16

Don't Expect to Shoot a 68

*"It took me 17 years to get 3,000 hits in baseball.
I did it in one afternoon on the golf course."*
— HANK AARON

A s I write earlier in this book, know your limitations and be realistic. In golf, there's no way most of us are going to shoot a 68, so get it out of your mind. Otherwise, you're going to be very disappointed.

The best score I've ever shot was a 79, and that was only once. I was thrilled. The next day I went and shot a 95. For most amateurs, the stars have to be aligned, and a lot of things have to break your way for you to get a great score. If your attitude is good and you're feeling good, you'll usually find yourself playing well. You know the scene: that rare day when you go out there and everything is clicking, it's not raining, it's a nice cool day, and the green is breaking just right. Even your bad shots are good!

That's when you do relatively well, but it's not always going to be that way.

Looking down the Course

As I've stated earlier in this book, managing your expectations in golf is important, and it's even more critical in wealth management. When you sit down with a reliable expert who has developed a solid financial plan for you, you'll see that it is always about getting back to the basics—not getting away from what got you to where you are.

When you set up the fundamentals of your plan—all of the criteria—you are taking the approach of saying, "This is what I want to accomplish over a certain time period, and this is the risk I am willing to take to get there."

It is amazing that in review meetings during a market downturn, many people focus on the immediate situation at hand, as opposed to looking at the overall plan to see if they are still on track.

If the market is down this year, that's just this one year. You're still accomplishing your goals. That's managing expectations successfully.

If you came in tomorrow and said, "I want to give you $10 million, and I need to get a 15 percent rate of return," We would say you were in the wrong place, since that is not realistic. So don't wish for something that's almost impossible to accomplish.

Somewhere, you should have a written investment policy statement (IPS) that outlines your objectives, time horizon and the amount of risk you are willing to take. This profile will help to determine your asset allocation and the types of investments that are most suitable for you. (For more on this, see Chapter 4, "Develop Your Strategy.")

Chasing performance or reaching for yield may subject you to taking on more risk without you knowing it.

Periodic reference to your IPS should keep you on track and help manage your expectations.

If you manage your expectations successfully—not expecting that 68—you should do just fine.

Chapter 17

Choose Your Shots Carefully

"If you watch a game, it's fun. If you play at it, it's recreation. If you work at it, it's golf."
— BOB HOPE

I n golf, every situation on the course can be totally unique. There are literally thousands of different opportunities and hazards that face you as you move down the course, and these will change to some degree every time you go out there. (Hmmm, sounds like financial planning, doesn't it?)

This means that you have to choose your shots carefully as you move from hole to hole. Here, I'll talk about a couple of the more common decisions, and how they relate to successfully managing your wealth.

Taking What You Can Control

There are certain times you should execute a strategy that you know you can control, even if it doesn't appear expedient or promise maximum returns. For example, you hit your ball into the woods. You have a couple of choices:

One shot would be to go through a big opening that happens to be off your line to the green by 90 degrees. You would just need to take a wedge and chip the ball out there, at which point you'd be behind one shot.

The other option you could take would be straight ahead, but there might be 15 trees in the way. I have seen more people than not trying to go through the 15 trees. (They say a tree is 90 percent air, so is a screen door, right?!) If you try that shot, 90 percent of the time you will hit one of the trees, and you will be worse off than you were before.

Here's something a guy said to me once, and it has always stuck in my head: "Remember, the guy taking this shot is the guy who took the shot before this one."

More often than not, golfers score better if they don't take that crazy shot. Think about that when planning your financial future.

Know When to Lay Up

Knowing when to lay up is another related key to your strategy—both on the golf course and in your financial planning. Again, it comes down to how much risk you are willing to take, and whether the reward is worth it.

Use your averages in order to determine how far you can hit the ball with two good shots. For example, suppose I hit a 240-yard drive on a 470-yard par 5. I may be tempted to hit with my 3-wood, which could drive the ball another 200 yards, but I also think:

a) Maybe this is the time I'll hit it "pure" and I'll get in on the green, or

b) If I don't get that distance, I'll be real close for a "chip and a putt."

But a lot of things could happen with that 3-wood— a slice, a hook, etc. So even if I do hit it well (around 200 yards), how comfortable am I with that 30-yard chip? Are there any green-side bunkers, fescue, or thick rough?

Perhaps I'd be better off leaving that 3-wood in my bag and playing it as a 3-shot hole using a club that will give me my "go-to" third shot—perhaps a pitching wedge to the green.

So, instead of going for greatness (which I may achieve three out of 10 times), I avoid those extra strokes if I don't hit it "on the screws," and play it safe with two clubs I can control more and can wield with more confidence.

Assessing the situation and choosing the right strategy can help increase the probability of getting on in regulation (on the green so that you can two-putt for par.)

There are times in our financial lives where it makes sense to "lay up" as well. Sometimes the tips you get from your neighbors or friends at a cocktail party seem so tempting, and you really want to "go for it." Yes, that tip could be "The One" that doubles or even triples your money, but in reality, these things come with a lot of risk—and of course I'm talking about losing your money!

So, if you can't afford the loss, you may want to "lay up" and invest somewhere safer with fewer potential hazards. It's a shot that you should choose carefully.

Now, having said that, I can assure you that the next time some of us are confronted with that same situation, the first reaction will be to go for it. I suppose it's human nature, or testosterone, or something like that. Playing on a muni course some time ago, I was confronted with a make-or-break, almost impossible shot. What happened next is something I'll never forget as long as I live: My opponent says to me, "A scared man can't make no money!"

Well, you can probably guess where this is going. I took this incredibly high-risk shot that was well above my abilities. To borrow yet another sports metaphor, I swung for the fences. (Or, you could even say, I "came out of my shoes." Okay…enough.)

The outcome? Well let's just say wasn't pretty. Still, I learned some good lessons that day: one, know your abilities; two, swinging hard usually equals very bad results; and three, whenever someone says to you, "A scared man can't make no money," think twice before your next move!

Chapter 18

Have a Team

> *"Great things in business are never done by one person.*
> *They're done by a team of people."*
> — STEVE JOBS

Earlier in this book I discussed the importance of working with a pro to improve both your golf game and financial planning strategy. I think that's really important advice, but you actually need more help than that if you want to maximize your success.

In golf, getting multiple experts to help you with your game is a big thing now. Besides having a pro teach you how to properly grip the club and proper mechanics of the swing, there are specific fitness programs for flexibility to further build up your control and stamina, improve your swing range, and build greater acceleration and force.

You also can have your local pro talk to you about equipment, and of course you have a caddy that helps you to strategize and choose the right clubs when you're out on the course.

All of these people truly are part of your team, and they make you better at the game. Likewise, you need a financial team to work with you so that you can get the most out of that most important pursuit and achieve better results.

Creating Your Financial Team

We create financial teams for our clients all the time. We start by asking each one this question: "When was the last time your lawyer, your banker, your accountant, your insurance agent and your financial advisor were in the same room talking about you?"

You probably know what the answer always is. *Never!* And I'm talking about people who have a lot of money, have retirement and estate issues, tax concerns, and all kinds of other considerations.

The reality is, of course, that usually you're not going to get all of these people in the same room at the same time, but somebody needs to coordinate that effort, and at least get everybody on the same page. Usually it is the financial advisor, but whoever assumes that role becomes an invaluable player on your team. Remember, you are always the team owner, and the rest are coaches, managers, and key players—all there to help you achieve your dream.

The other day a client and I were talking about financial issues, and in that room happened to be her real estate manager and her accountant. I've had many meetings like this, because everyone doesn't know the same thing, or have the same expertise. Most people are most knowledgeable in one area, but not so much the others. Their efforts need to be coordinated for maximum positive impact on your financial strategy.

I had a situation where a successful client came in to talk about his estate. He had a $5 million insurance policy that he owned personally, which is a big disadvantage in estate planning because of the tax and inheritance consequences—but a lot of people just don't understand that.

I asked him why he owned this insurance personally. He answered, "I don't know. The insurance person just sold it to me."

I said, "Do you realize that if you had this in a an irrevocable life insurance trust (ILIT), trust, it would be excluded from your taxable estate? Here you are trying to provide liquidity, but that $5 million is compounding your problem, because it's adding to the value of your estate, which is going to be taxed."

Let's say your net estate is $10 million. In addition to that, you have a $5 million insurance policy that you own. So, your net estate for federal estate tax purposes is $15 million. There is a $5.450 million exemption ($10.9 million if you are married). Supposing you are married, your net estate would be $4.1 million, subject to federal estate tax. If the insurance is owned by an irrevocable trust (which is a very simple and inexpensive thing to create) that $5 million dollars would be excluded from your estate, making the estate less than the $10.9 million exemption, thus having a ZERO federal estate tax. Depending on your state of residence, you may still be subject to the state estate tax.

(However, keep in mind that this is a generalized description. Your specific situation may be much more complex.)

So why did this person have a $5 million life insurance policy owned personally, subject to estate tax, in the first place?

Doing It Right from the Beginning

With a team, you would probably avoid a disaster like this. It's much easier when you do things correctly from the beginning. Remember: Measure twice and cut once to avoid having a problem in the future. It's much easier to assure that happens when people work together to find the best solution.

The old saying is, "Two heads are better than one." The truth is that three or four heads may be even better than two when it comes to wealth management.

Today it is virtually impossible for one person to be an expert in all areas. We work with a team of CPAs, CFP®s, CFA®s, attorneys, insurance, and real estate professionals on behalf of our clients. Each brings a specific value to the table so that all of the quantitative and qualitative issues are properly addressed.

I've worked with some of the most brilliant people in this business, and yet every once in a while one might get lost between the "forest and the trees." That's when another team member usually jumps in and offers advice that creates the proverbial "perfect" solution.

It is critical that the team is made up of people with different disciplines and expertise. Again, this is another area where diversification comes into play.

Introduce your team to everyone important to you: your spouse, children, guardians, trustees, advisors, and others. All of the team members' contact information should be on one page, reviewed periodically, and distributed to those who may need it.

You also should put together a one-page "document locator:" a hit list of where to find wills or trusts, bank accounts, brokerage accounts, insurance policies, and other key papers.

Ultimately, your golf team—your pro, your caddy, and even your personal trainer—is focused on getting you better outcomes. That is exactly what your financial team should offer you as well. Why would you approach it any other way?

Chapter 19

Become a Lifelong Student of the Game

"That's the type of person I remember: a student of the game."
— ERNIE CHATMAN

So now you've reached the 19th hole of this little outing. I had some fun. How about you?

Sit back and enjoy a beverage. You've earned it. But remember that you can never rest on your laurels with golf, financial planning, or life itself. You have to keep learning and improving.

I love learning something new every day, whatever it is. Being a student of the game means you have to know a little bit of history, the nuances, the trivia, the proper technique, the latest equipment—all will give you a deeper understanding of where you want to go and how you will get there.

In golf, there are rules, as with any other sport, but so many people have no idea what the rules are. If you want to be successful, you need to watch carefully. You can watch somebody and say, "Wow look at that! What are you doing? I'm going to see if I can pull that off."

In wealth management it's the same thing. You become a student, and you need to know enough so that you can at least understand what we're talking about.

One of the most important characteristics you should look for in a financial advisor is his or her ability to listen. As easy as that may sound, you'd be surprised how many people have poor listening skills.

A great example of this is when you go to your doctor. He doesn't start by telling you how great he is, how many patients he has, or what latest medicines he has to offer. As a matter of fact, if he started off by giving you a prescription before the examination, you'd probably run out of his office.

Instead he probably starts by asking, "Why are you here?" or, "What's bothering you?" So wouldn't your financial advisor be focused on the same concerns…in other words, YOU!?

Some fellow golfers and financial clients want to know enough so that they can do their financial planning themselves, and that's fine. It certainly works for some. Others seek some level of advice, from "just show me the basics" to "please help me from A to Z."

Understand Your Tools and Strategies

To whatever extent you or an advisor manage your financial affairs, make sure that you fully understand your strategy and your tools every step of the way. I would never tell anybody to do anything that they don't understand. If you were my client, and you were confused about some aspect of your plan, we would tell you to stop and take a step back. Then I'd explain it again and put it in terms you could absorb. Some folks get it right away; for others it may take a while.

We asked so many people, "Why are you investing in this way?" "I don't know," they say. "This other person told me to do it that way."

Would you want to take that approach with your doctor?

"So, why are you getting an operation?"

"I don't know."

You would never do that when it comes to your health, nor would you take the know-nothing approach in so many other facets of your life—so why do you even consider doing it when it comes to your investments and financial choices?

Keep Investing for the Future

Investing for the future shouldn't stop when you retire. To make your money work for you throughout your retirement years, keep investing. Keep in touch with your team and put their collective knowledge at your fingertips. Study the successes of others. Ask questions. Read and keep current. Understand *why* you are investing so that you will stick to your plan. Always gather research so you do not miss excellent investment opportunities, and remain flexible—be ready to make adjustments when required.

You never stop learning. Whether it's about golf, financial planning, or life in general, all of us should always continue to learn something—whatever that something is.

No Mulligans

When I first heard the word "mulligan," I thought "what a great idea!" Of course, a mulligan is that extra stroke allowed after a poor shot, not counted on the scorecard. In other words, it's a "do-over."

In reality, once you start playing serious golf, there are no mulligans. It's just like in life—you don't get to take a mulligan when you hit a "poor shot."

That doesn't mean you don't get a "second chance" at anything, and all of us do get to learn from our mistakes, but make no mistake about it: None of us gets to take a mulligan!

That's why it's so important for you to think before you act, analyzing each situation before you react. You are accountable and responsible for every decision you make and every action you take.

As Bobby Jones once said, "Golf is the closest game to the game we call life. You get bad breaks from good shots, you get good breaks from bad shots—but you have to play the ball where it lies."

So, I urge you to go out and play the round of your life!

Index

401(k)
asset distribution, 17
investment time horizons, 39–40

403(b)
investment time horizons, 39–40

A
Advisors. *See* Financial advisors
Asset distribution
    401(k), 17, 39–40
    403(b), 39–40
    business owners, 18
    cash balance plans, 39–40
    defined benefit plans, 39–40
    IRA, 17, 39–40
    joint tenants with rights of survivorship (JTWROS), 17
    life insurance, 17
    pensions, 39–40
    profit sharing, 39–40
    retirement plans, 39–40
    tenants in common (TIC), 17
    trusts, 17

B
Believe in yourself, 1–2
Buffett, Warren
    patience, 70

Eye on the ball, 47–50
  See also Discipline; Focus

F

Family considerations
  estate planning, 19
Feel, 34
Financial advisors
  creating a team, 81–85
  periodic portfolio review, 53–54
  responsibilities, 23–25, 30, 82, 88
Financial planning
  cadence, 34–36
  cash flow analysis, 44–45
  creating a team, 81–85
  discipline, 49–50
  document locator, 85
  education, 36, 87–91
  emergency fund, 60
  estate planning, 17–19
  focus, 47–49
  implementation, 51–54
    periodic portfolio review, 53–54
  investment time horizons, 37–41, 89–90
  mental flexibility, 66–67
  monitoring, 23–25
  qualitative analysis, 23
  quantitative analysis, 23
  starting out, 10–12
Financial products
  income generation, 30
  retirement plans, 39–40
  selection process, 27–31
Financial team. *See* Financial advisors
Flexibility
  mental, 66–67
  physical, 64–65
Focus, 47–49
Follow-through, 51–54
  See also Implementation

example situation, 83–84
Long game, 37–41
    See also Investment time horizons
Long term. *See* Investment time horizons

M
Mulligan, 90–91

P
Patience, 69–72
    Buffett, Warren, 70
    stay the course, 70–71
    Templeton, Sir John, 71
    "this time it's different," 71–72
    See also Cadence
Pensions
    asset distribution, 39–40
Periodic portfolio review, 53–54
Personal risk assessment, 57
Practice, 33–36
    feel, 34
Profit sharing
    asset distribution, 39–40

Q
Qualitative analysis
    financial plan, 23
Quantitative analysis
    financial plan, 23

R
Required minimum distribution, 40
    See also Retirement plans
Retirement plans, 39–40
Risk management, 12–13, 55–58
    decision making, 77–80
    diversification, 56–57, 59–62
    insurance, 13, 58
    investment time horizons, 37–41, 89–90
    personal risk assessment, 57
RMD. *See* Required minimum distribution

Credits

Publisher/Editorial Director: Michael Roney

Art Director/Illustrations: Sarah M. Clarehart

Copyeditor/Proofreader: Maya Ziobro

Indexer: Karl Ackley

Contact: info@highpointpubs.com

HIGHPOINT
EXECUTIVE
PUBLISHING

www.highpointpubs.com